DR. MYLES MUNROE

KEYS *for* MEN

WHITAKER
HOUSE

KEYS FOR MEN

ISBN: 978-1-60374-152-1
Printed in the United States of America
© 2009 by Dr. Myles Munroe

Dr. Myles Munroe
Bahamas Faith Ministries International
P.O. Box N9583
Nassau, Bahamas
E-mail: bfmadmin@bfmmm.com
www.bfmmm.com; www.bfmi.tv; www.mylesmunroe.tv

Whitaker House
1030 Hunt Valley Circle
New Kensington, PA 15068
www.whitakerhouse.com

1 2 3 4 5 6 7 8 9 10 11 12 🅦 17 16 15 14 13 12 11 10 09

INTRODUCTION

*W*hat is real manhood? How are men and women meant to relate to one another? How can men be effective husbands and fathers? Contemporary concepts of maleness are often ambiguous. They also tend to focus on roles rather than on the male's underlying *purpose*—a crucial distinction. Some would like to dismiss males as hopelessly aggressive and domineering, with a nature in need of an overhaul.

All the above issues reflect a crisis of *identity*. What does it mean to be male? The true nature of the male can be determined only by returning to the original process of his creation, based on the premise that no one knows a product like its manufacturer. It is imperative that the male rediscover his original purpose in God and understand his true potential, as well as gain a clear understanding of his principal function within the human family.

Through *Keys for Men*, you can discover God's vital purpose for the male, the complementary roles of males and females, and how you, as a man, can build a better life for yourself, your family, your community, and your nation.

—Dr. Myles Munroe

Literature focusing on changes in men's lives has indicated that the male is in a state of crisis and internal conflict. Without a clear idea of their identity, men are trying to cope with the collision of new societal expectations and traditional ideas of what a man should be.

What men really need to discover is their underlying purpose. A man's position and actions must flow out of his purpose, not the other way around.

To discover the purpose of something, never ask the creation; ask the creator. We find our purpose only in the mind of our Maker.

$\mathcal{G}$od created everything with a purpose, and His purpose is the key to our fulfillment. The purpose of something determines its nature, design, and features. What God plans is intentional, meaningful, and guaranteed to succeed.

*I*f males understand the purpose and responsibilities God has given them and the true design of their relationships with females, they can be free to fulfill their destinies and potentials. They can be the men they were created to be.

*M*en's underlying purpose transcends culture and tradition. Knowledge of what it means to be a true man cannot be acquired by observing the confused culture around us.

*M*en must adopt an entirely new way of thinking. They need to think in terms of *inherent purpose* rather than *roles*. Roles have never been the true basis of a male's identity and worth. Roles can be helpful or harmful, but ultimately they merely reflect culture and tradition.

*I*f males are going to fulfill their purpose as men, husbands, and fathers, they must rediscover God's plan for them. Otherwise, they will hurt those around them, even if it's unintentional. Where purpose is not known, abuse is inevitable.

*G*od has given males a unique leadership influence. The male is the key to building strong, enduring social infrastructures, stable families, sane societies, and secure nations. As the man goes, so goes the family, the society, and the world.

What is a "real man"? Someone who knows the reality of who he is and lives in that reality. This knowledge starts with understanding the significance of being created purposefully by God.

God created every man with a purpose. It is possible to do good things but not the things that are best based on God's purposes for you.

Good deeds are not a substitute for rightness. Knowing and fulfilling your purpose is the only way to do what is right.

KEYS for MEN

*M*ales are not divine experiments.
When God created them, He had already
predetermined what men were
supposed to be and do.

Since God created everything with a purpose, men need to go to Him if they want to know their true reason for being. If they try to change His plans, they are in essence fighting against themselves and the way they were designed to function.

If a man wants to know his reason for living, he must look to God and His Manual—the Bible—not to other males. If he looks to himself or others, he will travel an unreliable and hazardous course in life.

A man will fulfill his purpose only if he seeks the mind of his Maker with all his heart. When God's plans unfold before him, his fragmented life will become an orderly whole, and he will become the man he was meant to be.

The answer for males in the twenty-first century is to (1) define their worth based on God's purpose rather than society's roles, (2) learn God's vision for their lives, and (3) continue to live in the truth of who they were created to be.

*A*man may be able to see the outcome of God's purposes in his life twenty years into the future or only one day ahead. Yet if he is living in God's plans for him, he has found the key to his existence.

When God made man, He essentially drew man out of Himself, so that the essence of man would be just like Him. Since *"God is spirit"* (John 4:24), He created man as spirit, and spirit is eternal.

$\mathscr{M}$an is the reason for the universe. I didn't say man is the center of it. God is the center of everything.

God's plan of creation was this: as God ruled the unseen realm in heaven, man would rule the visible realm on earth, with God and man enjoying continual communion through their spiritual natures.

*G*od doesn't want man to work *for* Him; He wants man to work *with* Him. The Bible says that we are *"God's fellow workers"* (2 Corinthians 6:1).

God created man in his own image, in the image of God he created him; male and female he created them" (Genesis 1:27). After God created man—the spiritual being made in His image—He placed man in two physical "houses": male and female.

God designed and equipped the male to carry out every purpose and function he has been given.

The purpose of man—the spiritual being—and the purpose of the male—the physical being—are two different things. The male was made to serve the needs of mankind on earth and to enable mankind to fulfill its purpose.

The male was designed by God to be the foundation of the human family. The woman came out of the man rather than the earth because she was designed to have the male as her support.

When men have cracks in the substructures of their lives, if they don't learn what it means to be a strong foundation in God, then their families and others whom they influence can find themselves on shaky ground.

When God made the male first,
He wasn't saying that the male is more
important than the female. He was saying
that the male has a specific responsibility.

The purpose of the male is to give foundation to the structure of life. Even though the foundation is important, it's not more important than the other parts of the building.

$\mathcal{M}$en need to live like the foundation they were created to be. Just be there and keep the home steady so that your family can always lean on you and know that you aren't going to crack.

*M*en, whenever you allow a negative history to predict your future, your present is in trouble. What we are about is *creating* history.

*I*t doesn't matter who your grandfather was. The important issue is what your *grandchildren* are going to say about you.

A good man doesn't leave an inheritance of just money and land. He leaves a heritage, something to stand on, something to lean on throughout life.

Man's priority in creation means not only that he was designed to be the foundation of the human family, but also that he was the first to have a relationship with God, to experience God's creation, and to receive God's instructions.

The primary purpose of the male is to be in God's presence; he is not wired to function outside the presence of the Lord.

The male's purpose was chosen by God, and it may be summed up as *his priority*, *his position*, and *his assignment*.

$\mathcal{T}$he male's *priority* means that he was formed first in order to be the foundation of the human family.

The male's *position* means that he is to remain continually in God's presence. Without doing this, he cannot function in God's purposes.

*T*he male's *assignment* reveals six specific purposes that God created the man to fulfill: *visionary*, *leader*, *teacher*, *cultivator*, *provider*, and *protector*.

$\mathcal{M}$en, being a provider means supplying not only financial support but also emotional and intellectual support.

God never intended for Adam to move from the garden of Eden. He intended for the *garden to move over the earth*. God wanted Adam to take the presence of the garden and spread it throughout the world.

The problem with many of us men is that we think we don't need God when, in fact, He's the first thing we need.

What was the first thing that God gave the male? He didn't give him a woman, a job, or even a command; He gave him His presence.

*I*t isn't enough just to go to church. We need to be in touch with God constantly, hearing His voice, listening to His commands, and following His direction.

*G*od built into the male a need for His presence. That is why all men are searching for God in one way or another, whether they acknowledge it or not.

$\mathscr{G}$od originally intended for man to grow in dominion ability by learning to dominate the area in which he was placed.

*G*od doesn't give us more than we can
handle. He always gives us just enough to
train us for the rest.

*I*t's dangerous to have everything,
all at once. God doesn't just promote us.
He qualifies us for promotion first.
If you've been faithful over a little, then
your responsibilities will be expanded to
much more. (See Matthew 25:14–23.)

The male was given the charge of being the visionary and leader—the one who would guide those who came after him in the ways of God. Everything that is necessary to lead the family is built into the male.

The male's purpose was not chosen by the male but by God. Whatever your purpose, that's where your position comes from.

Men, you are the responsible ones, whether you like it or not. If you run from your responsibility, it will run after you, because it's not just a role; it's a God-given purpose.

The nature of the work the male was given to do in the garden of Eden was not mindless labor—it was cultivation.

The purpose of the male is to develop
and cultivate both people and things
to God's glory.

Work exposes your potential. You cannot show what you have inside unless demands are made on it, and demands are placed on it by work.

God gave the male work because it is related to his purpose, which is to rule and manage what God has given him to do.

Even a man who knows and lives in his purpose is not complete, according to God. The male needs a companion or helper—not as a subordinate or a sidekick but as an equal partner with a complementary purpose.

Both single men and married men need women as fellow workers and colleagues in this world if they are to fulfill their purposes in life.

*I*f you as a man—whether married or single—believe that you don't need women, you are missing an important aspect of your existence.

The female is the male's perfect complement and equal partner in the purposes of God. She is the male's God-given companion. Everything about her is designed to help the man.

God created men and women to dominate the earth, not one another.

After the fall, both the man and the woman still ruled, but their relationship was distorted. Instead of equality, there was imbalance.

$\mathscr{S}$atan is afraid of the power that would be released through a man and woman united in God's purposes.

*T*hroughout history, a controlling tendency has particularly undermined the male's true purpose and has resulted in the widespread devaluing of women—preventing both men and women from fulfilling their purposes in God.

$\mathcal{M}$uch of a man's tendency to control comes from a false understanding of how his own nature is to function in dominion. In its true form, the male ego is not negative but positive. The problem is that the male's passion to prove his strength has been perverted and abused by Satan and the sinful nature.

*M*any men have muscle but are weak in their minds, hearts, disciplines, responsibilities, and spirits. That is why they feel the need for excess muscle—to hide their weakness in these other areas.

A strong man is a man who understands his God-given strength—a man who has fully maximized his potential for the purpose for which he was created.

*W*henever you take your position
by force, you've moved out of your
legal standing.

*A*ny time a man starts to dominate another human being, he is out of God's will. Men were created to dominate the earth, not one another. When this occurs, and power is abused, then authority is forfeited.

*A*ny man who has to force a woman to submit does not deserve to be submitted to. He is no longer worthy of submission; he has become a slave driver.

Perfect love drives out fear" (1 John 4:18). This means that if a man has to make a woman afraid of him in order to force her to do something he wants done, then he doesn't know what love is.

*W*e follow Jesus because He knows where He's going, He knows how to get there, He's the only Way there, and we like where He's going. Most of all, His love draws us to Him.

$\mathcal{D}$on't quote Scripture to a woman unless you are behaving like Jesus did. When you start acting like Jesus, you won't have to demand that your wife submit.

$\mathcal{W}$hen you start loving your wife like Jesus loves her, when you start forgiving her like Jesus forgives her, when you start caring for her and listening to her like Jesus does, she will do anything for you—because she wants a man like Jesus in the house.

*J*esus never once commanded anybody to follow Him. He always asked, because He knew who He was and where He was going.

*I*f a male wants to be a true leader, he must learn who he is in God and become someone who earns respect—someone who loves, guides, and inspires rather than forces others to do what he wants.

God isn't going to abandon the male's leadership responsibility for the sake of changing cultural attitudes toward gender roles.

*I*f men would realize that dominion is to be exercised over the world and not over other people, that men and women are equal but different, and that men and women need one another, we would go a long way toward restoring both harmonious relationships between males and females and God's plan for humanity.

$\mathcal{T}$here can be no true dominion over the earth unless God's original design is intact. The way we are designed is because of our purpose for existence.

$\mathscr{G}$od's plan is for the individual strengths of men and women to combine to produce exponential results—outcomes much greater than either could accomplish alone.

$\mathcal{B}$eing a visionary is a foundational responsibility for the male because, without it, he can't fulfill his other assignments of leader, teacher, cultivator, provider, and protector.

To have vision means to be able
to conceive of and move toward
your purpose in life.

The only way you can discover your vision is to listen to what God is saying to you. God has a vision for every male because the male was *created* to be a visionary.

$\mathcal{T}$he male is *designed* to be a visionary. He is able to look at the big picture in life and to plan for the future from a logical, practical standpoint.

$\mathcal{G}$od always provides for the vision He gives. Your responsibility is to support and sustain the vision until it comes to fruition.

*H*aving vision means that you can already see the end of your purpose. It means that you have faith in God and what He has told you to do so that you are continually moving toward your vision as it is moving toward you.

*I*f you look at God's pattern in the Bible, the man is given the vision, but the woman is there to make sure that he accomplishes it.

KEYS for MEN

$\mathcal{M}$any men don't have a vision for their lives because they are not committed to God and to seeking His will in this area. If a man does not have a relationship with God, he cannot fully function in his purpose.

*T*he example Jesus set for us by His life shows us our need for these important elements related to purpose: a clear self-image and a life consistent with one's purpose and calling.

True vision can be found only in God's presence. Jesus Himself was in constant contact with the Father in order to know how to fulfill His life's purpose.

The most important thing a male can do is to acknowledge the headship of Christ and commit to following Him on a daily basis in order to receive His direction.

You aren't fulfilling your purpose as a man until you can hear the voice of God. You aren't fulfilling your purpose as a man until you start speaking and affirming the Word of God in your life.

*I*f we want to fulfill our dominion responsibilities and assignments, we have to do so through the Spirit of Christ as we follow God's will.

Men are to function as priests in their homes. They need to stay close to God so they can tell their families what God is saying to them.

*A*man needs a clear vision of these three things: (1) who he is in God, (2) what his overall purpose as a male is, and (3) what his purpose as an individual man is.

*N*o man has the right to lead a woman
if he doesn't have the ability to hear God.
"Where there is no vision, the people perish"
(Proverbs 29:18 KJV).

$\mathscr{M}$en need vision even before discipline, because discipline comes from vision. Discipline comes as you plan ahead and make sacrifices to fulfill your vision.

God is concerned with men who have visions from Him and who can support, sustain, and nurture their families and others as they move toward these visions in pursuit of His purposes.

The male is not the head of his home because he has to lead. He has to lead because he *is* the head. His position is inherent.

The male was designed for *responsible* leadership. He is to lead and be responsible for everything under his jurisdiction.

A real man doesn't ignore authority. He remains in the garden of God's presence, praying and reading God's Word, so that he may understand and obey His commands.

God is not looking for a controller. He is looking for a leader who makes himself fruitful by being pruned when necessary in order to yield a healthier and greater harvest.

The male was created to be the spiritual leader and teacher of his family. The male has been designed with the capacity to fulfill his purpose of teaching.

*I*f a man doesn't have the knowledge and capability to teach his family the Word of God, then he is not really ready for marriage. Do you know the Word? Make it a priority to study and gain knowledge of the Bible.

*I*f you want God to consider you His friend, then become a teacher in your home. You have to be full of the Word in order to give it to your family.

$\mathcal{I}$f you can take care of your children, then God says, "All right, now you can lead My church." If you can manage your home, then you can manage the house of God.

You cannot teach something if you're not being an example of it yourself. A good teacher is one who teaches by example.

A father should help his children discover their gifts and talents. He should affirm their accomplishments and tell them what they can become in life, so they can have positive outlooks based on faith in God.

*I*f a man is to love his wife as Christ loves the church, he needs to be filled with the Word, just as Christ is filled with the Word.

The male has been given the serious but exciting responsibility of shaping the lives of his family members for the better. In this way, he is a partner with God in fulfilling His plan of creation.

$\mathcal{G}$od has given men the ability to provide for and protect everything He has entrusted to their care.

The two dominion assignments of provider and protector are interrelated because they work together to enable a man to secure himself and those who are under his care.

Some men have forgotten that worship takes precedence over work. When your work interferes with your worship, you cease to fulfill the purpose of a real man.

A provider anticipates needs before they arrive. A loving husband is always thinking about what his wife is going to need tomorrow, and he plans for it today.

God designed the male to gain satisfaction from both working and providing. When he's able to do these two things, he's a happy man.

A man doesn't need to be married to be responsible for women. Start being the protector of every female who comes into your presence, because you were created to be responsible for her.

God gave men a drive to excel so they can be good examples for their children of how to be faithful during tough times. God gave men egos so they can constantly come forth with more motivation and more hope for life's battles.

A male doesn't decide to work—he's designed to work. He doesn't decide to teach—he's required to teach. There is no fulfillment without satisfying your purpose.

*M*an was given work before the woman was created. This means that before a man needs a woman, and before he is ready for marriage, he needs work.

$\mathcal{G}$od designed men and women as sexual beings. He created sex and said that it is *"very good"* (Genesis 1:31). God is negative only about the misuse of sex.

Marriage enables us to enjoy sex to the fullest. There is so much freedom within the laws of God. Yet when you violate God's laws, the first thing you lose is your peace.

Remember that sex is a physical sign of a spiritual act—the giving of oneself completely to another and for another. Marital love is the binding of one spouse to another.

As Christian men, we need to teach young men that sexual attraction is physiological and shouldn't be acted upon outside the marriage relationship.

The answer to questions about sex is: behave yourself. End of discussion. Don't let a woman take advantage of you—and make sure you don't take advantage of a woman's feelings for you.

*B*e careful how you respond to a woman's praise and attention. If it is starting to lead to inappropriate attraction, you know you need to back off.

God has given the female certain strengths that the male does not possess. Until the male recognizes the female's God-given strengths, he will be weak in those areas, because she is designed to supply what he lacks.

When men expect women to think, react, and behave in the same ways they do—that is, when they don't know or appreciate their God-given differences—they will experience conflict with women.

*W*hen men and women understand
and value one another's purposes, they can
have rewarding relationships, and they
can blend their unique designs
harmoniously for God's glory.

The primary needs of males are respect, recreational companionship, and sex. The primary needs of females are love, conversation, and affection.

A single man needs respect as much as a married man does. He needs the sisterly affirmation of female relatives and friends if he is to feel fulfilled as a man.

When a married couple shares important aspects of their lives with each other, they build understanding, companionship, and intimacy in their marriage.

A male needs to share his interests, and a female needs conversation; these related needs can be a wonderful bridge of communication between men and women.

$\mathcal{W}$hen a male speaks, it is generally an expression of what he is *thinking*. When a female speaks, it is usually an expression of what she is *feeling*. They are communicating two different types of information.

$\mathcal{M}$en and women can eliminate
much frustration in their relationships
by understanding each other's problem-
solving strengths and using them to
benefit one another.

*N*o one person, and no one gender, can look at the world with complete perspective. Therefore, God has designed the male and female to live and work together in unity for a wiser and richer experience of life.

KEYS *for* MEN

*I*f you want to be blessed, don't focus on your needs but discover what the other person's needs are and seek to fulfill them.

A father is meant to represent the fatherhood of God to his children.

Men, we have a tremendous calling ahead of us to change not only our own perspectives of fatherhood, but also those of our sons. We have to communicate to them the standards of God.

The greatest heritage a man can leave his sons and daughters is not money or property, but faith.

*B*uying things for your kids doesn't necessarily mean you love them. Love is not buying gifts. Love is *you being a gift*.

Love also means correcting, chastening, and reproving your children when they need it. Children are begging to be corrected, but many fathers don't have the sense to realize it.

A father needs to read and study the Word of God so he can teach it to his children. It's impossible to teach something you haven't learned yourself.

It was I who taught Ephraim to walk" (Hosea 11:3). Our heavenly Father takes a personal interest in our training. Likewise, we are to train our children personally.

*Y*our children need discipline, which involves instilling moral and mental character in them and giving them values. You don't give values just by punishing. You give values by correcting.

Comfort your children by letting them know they are loved, even when they make mistakes or don't live up to your expectations. Listen to their struggles and problems with kindness and understanding. Give them warm embraces and loving words when they are sad.

To be a comforter, you have to be accessible to your children. You have to know what's going on in their lives so you can know when they're going through struggles and loneliness.

As you imitate your heavenly Father, your children will imitate you and reflect the character and life of their Creator. That is what the dominion assignment of fatherhood is all about.

*Y*ou are born a male, but you have to become a man. To become a real man, a male needs to understand that God's purposes must permeate his entire life so they can overflow into the lives of others.

A real man wants to be spiritually renewed so that the fullness of God's image and likeness is restored to his life.

A real man aspires to work and to develop his gifts and talents. A real man's motivation for work is to fulfill the purposes for which he was created.

A real man endeavors to encourage others to reflect the image and creativity of God in all they are and do—spiritually, emotionally, psychologically, and physically.

A real man exercises compassion, mercy, and justice. Through them, he shows true strength and brings the kingdom of God to others.

Men must understand that they are responsible for all their purpose assignments. The whole revelation has to hit you: "As a male, I am a visionary, leader, teacher, cultivator, provider, and protector."

Communities and nations will be transformed when men return to God and His purposes for them.

ABOUT THE AUTHOR

D.. Myles Munroe is an international motivational speaker, best-selling author, educator, leadership mentor, and consultant for government and business. Traveling extensively throughout the world, Dr. Munroe addresses critical issues affecting the full range of human, social, and spiritual development. The central theme of his message is the transformation of followers into leaders and the maximization of individual potential.

Founder and president of Bahamas Faith Ministries International (BFMI), a multidimensional organization headquartered in Nassau, Bahamas, Dr. Munroe is also the founder and executive producer of a number of radio and television programs aired worldwide. He has a B.A. from Oral Roberts University and an M.A. from the University of Tulsa and has been awarded a number of honorary doctoral degrees.

Dr. Munroe and his wife, Ruth, travel as a team and are involved in teaching seminars together. Both are leaders who minister with sensitive hearts and international vision. They are the proud parents of two college graduates, Charisa and Chairo (Myles Jr.).

For Information on Religious Tourism
e-mail: ljohnson@bahamas.com
1.800.224.3681

www.worship.bahamas.com

These inspirational quotes from best-selling author Dr. Myles Munroe
on leadership, single living, marriage, and prayer can be applied
to your life in powerful and practical ways.

Keys for Leadership: ISBN: 978-1-60374-029-6 • Gift • 160 pages
Keys for Living Single: ISBN: 978-1-60374-032-6 • Gift • 160 pages
Keys for Marriage: ISBN: 978-1-60374-030-2 • Gift • 160 pages
Keys for Prayer: ISBN: 978-1-60374-031-9 • Gift • 160 pages

WHITAKER
HOUSE